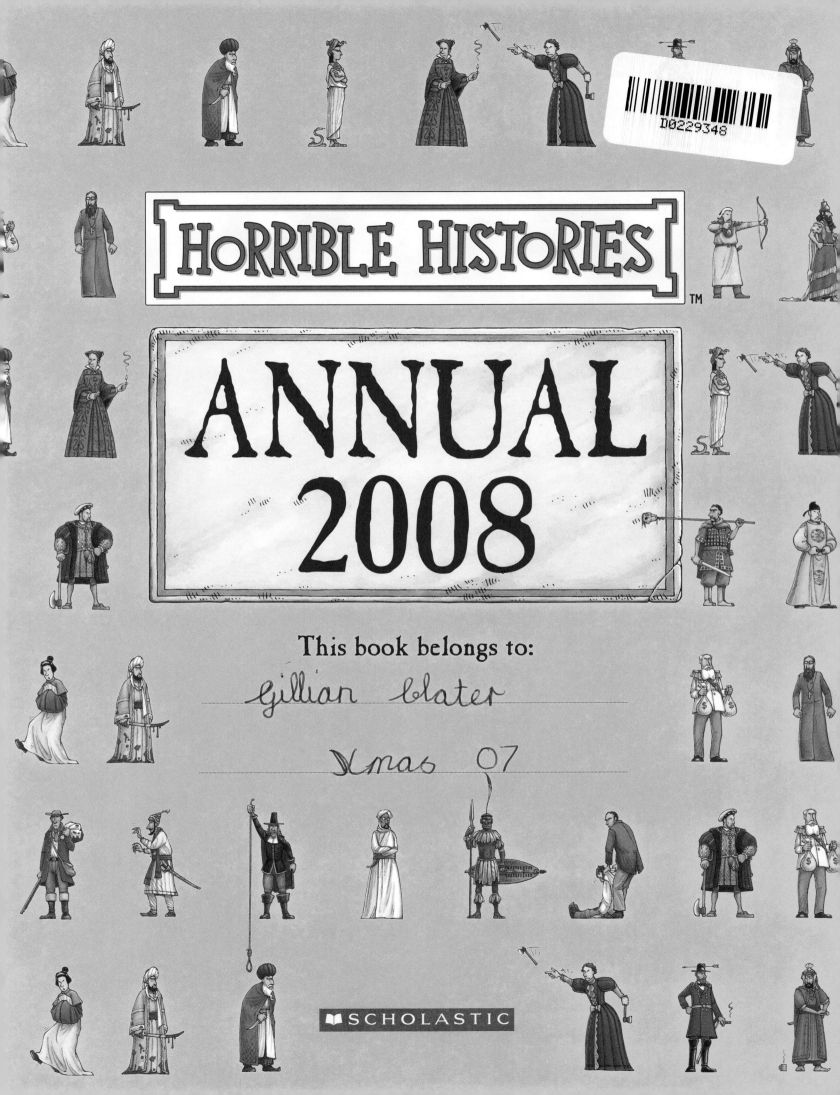

HORRIBLE HISTORIES™

ANNUAL 2008

This book belongs to:

Gillian blater

Xmas 07

SCHOLASTIC

Contents

COME ABOARD IF YOU DARE! BUT BE PREPARED FOR A VERY, VERY VILE VOYAGE!

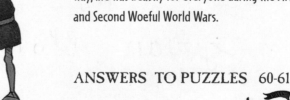

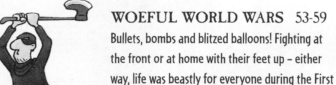

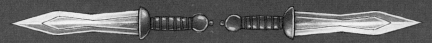

Horrible Hotspots

The awesome ancient world was one hot sizzling place you wouldn't want to visit – it was full of beastly battles, squabbling cities, crackpot kings, backstabbing politicians and gory games (mmm... times haven't changed much, have they?)

THE EGYPTIANS WERE FIERCE BUT FABULOUS, ESPECIALLY THE PHARAOHS. SOME EVEN OFFERED THEIR SERVANTS JOBS FOR LIFE WITH AMAZING TRAVEL OPPORTUNITIES! WHEN A PHARAOH DIED, HIS SERVANT COULD BE SACRIFICED SO THEY COULD TRAVEL TO THE AFTER-LIFE TOGETHER.

NO, NO, REALLY, I DON'T DESERVE THE TRIP OF AN AFTER-LIFETIME!

THEY MAY HAVE LOVED THEIR MUMMIES BUT THE AWESOME EGYPTIANS DIDN'T GET TO RULE A MIGHTY EMPIRE WITHOUT BEING FIERCE TOO. IN BATTLE, EGYPTIAN SOLDIERS HAD A HIDEOUS HABIT OF HACKING OFF THE RIGHT HAND OF EACH ENEMY'S CORPSE TO PROVE HOW MANY MEN THEY'D MASSACRED.

LET ME GIVE YOU A HAND

EVERYONE GOES ON ABOUT THE ANCIENT GREEKS BEING 'CIVILIZED', BUT THAT REALLY JUST MEANT THEY LIVED IN CITIES. SOME CITIES LIKE ATHENS WERE CULTURED AND CLEVER, WHILE OTHERS THOUGHT BEING TOUGH WAS TOPS. MOST OF ALL, THEY LIKED FIGHTING EACH OTHER.

YOUR CITY STINKS!

YOUR CITY STINKS

THE GREATEST GREEK OF THEM ALL WASN'T EVEN GREEK (OR EVEN THAT GREAT, COME TO THINK OF IT). ALEXANDER THE GREAT WAS IN FACT A MEAN MACEDONIAN. BUT HE DID STOP THE CITIES SCRAPPING AND TURNED GREECE INTO A MEGA-EMPIRE. ALEX WAS CONQUERING CRAZY. HE DECLARED HIMSELF GOD AND CARRIED ON EMPIRE-BUILDING UNTIL HE DROPPED DOWN DEAD FROM DRINK!

I AM A GOD! WORSHIP ME!

WELL, HE'S DEFINITELY IN TOUCH WITH THE SPIRITS

WITHIN A FEW CENTURIES, ALEX'S EMPIRE HAD BEEN TAKEN OVER BY GREECE'S RIVALS... THE ROTTEN ROMANS. THE ROMANS GAVE A YOUNG POLITICIAN CALLED JULIUS CAESAR AN ARMY AND SENT HIM INTO BATTLE. HE CONQUERED ALL OF GAUL (FRANCE) AND EVEN INVADED ENGLAND AND GERMANY. IN THE END HE GOT THE TOP JOB – RULER OF ROME. BUT SOME SENATORS THOUGHT THEY'D SHOW HIM WHAT A PAIN IN THE NECK HE'D BECOME...

DOES THIS MEAN YOU DON'T LIKE ME?!

THE ROTTEN ROMANS RULED THE ROOST FOR OVER 400 YEARS! AT THE HEIGHT OF THEIR GORY GLORY, THEY HELD THE GLADIATORIAL GAMES. 50,000 SPECTATORS WOULD PACK INTO THE COLOSSEUM IN ROME AND WATCH CRIMINALS AND SLAVES KILL EACH OTHER AND BE FED TO WILD BEASTS!

DON'T MAKE ANY QUICK DECISIONS. MULL IT OVER A WHILE, THINK ABOUT IT, TAKE YOUR TIME

Perilous Pyramids

It's believed the Egyptians used large ramps
to build their super-large pyramids. Unfortunately, they
didn't leave any records except for a list of
all the injuries that the pyramid-builders suffered!
So come on site, but mind your step...

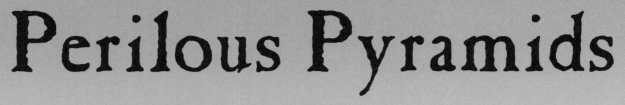

A lot of people think these pyramids were built by slaves. Wrong! They were built by farmers who were free for work when their lands were flooded each year by the River Nile.

The pharaoh inspected the work himself to check there was no slacking. Boo!

The workers had no excuses for turning up late – they lived in a large town right next to the building site! It was huge … but then again, it needed to be – it took thousands of men to build one of these things!

The wheel hadn't been invented when the Egyptians built their pyramids, so teams of men had to drag the colossal stones on sledges. Sometimes the men – and ropes – reached breaking point! Ouch!

The site hospitals were kept busy. Doctors mended broken bones, lopped off mangled limbs – and then sent you back to work!

The pharaoh's foremen made sure everyone worked HARDER and FASTER!

Workers ate bread and fish. They were paid partly in radishes and garlic, which kept them healthy but whiffy!

Mummy Misuse

Egyptians believed they needed their bodies in the afterlife. They would have been horrified to see what their remains were used for thousands of years later!

When Egyptians no longer believed that they needed an earthly body in the afterlife, they didn't need their mummies anymore! Mummies were exported to Europe to be chopped up and fed to sick people as cures. By the 16th century, the Egyptian government banned their export. Here are just some of the bizarre ways mummies were used … and misused!

As ornaments A display case with the hand or foot of a mummy became a very popular ornament for Victorian mantelpieces.

In witchcraft William Shakespeare knew about it: mummy is used as an ingredient of a witches' brew in the play *Macbeth*.

Foul Facts
In 19th-century America, mummy bandages were turned into brown paper, which was sold to butchers and grocers to be used as... wrapping for food! This caused an outbreak of deadly cholera. Many people died... the mummies' revenge?

As magic powder King Charles II (1630-1685) used to collect the dust and powder that fell from collections of mummies. He would rub this powder into his skin, all over. He believed that the ancient greatness of the mummies would rub off on him.

As fuel So many mummies were dug up in the 1800s that they became worthless. Some were burned as fuel for steam trains when wood and coal were in short supply! Poor people in Thebes even used the mummy bandages to heat their ovens.

In painting 16th-century artists believed that adding powdered mummy to their paint would stop it cracking when it dried.

Magic Powder	I HOPE THE POWDER DOESN'T RUB OFF BEFORE THE POWER RUBS OFF · RUB RUB
Fuel	THROW ANOTHER LEG ON THE FIRE, WOULD YOU DEAR
Ornaments	WE COULD ONLY AFFORD A KNEE
Witchcraft	NOT THAT KIND OF MUMMY!
Painting	

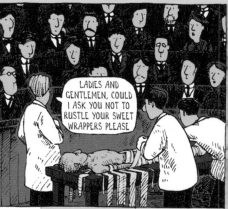

LADIES AND GENTLEMEN, COULD I ASK YOU NOT TO RUSTLE YOUR SWEET WRAPPERS PLEASE

For showbiz In Victorian England, people flocked to see a mummy being unwrapped! Doctor Pettigrew at the Royal College of Surgeons held the most popular unwrappings. Even on a bitterly cold January night, tickets were sold out and many important people could not get in. Refreshments were served after the performance.

...and some petrifying puzzles!

Song of the Nile

This song of the Nile, written by a priest of ancient Egypt, has lasted over 3,000 years. Can you choose the right words to finish it off?

① A) soak B) tickle C) feed

② A) rejoices B) stinks
   C) gets a bit wet

③ A) animals B) women
   C) camels

IF IT MOVES ... MUMMIFY IT

The Egyptians believed you had to mummify any creature you might need in the next world. Which of these creatures have been found mummified?

baboon

crocodile

sheep

ibis

snakes

Pyramid Numbers

Which number goes on the missing block to complete this puzzling pyramid?

Today the pyramids look like this...

But what did a newly built one look like?

A) Pyramid with 'step' sides turned into miniature gardens

B) Pyramid decorated with hieroglyphics (picture writing)

C) Pyramid with gleaming white smooth sides

That's Blown It!

August 24, AD 79 was a scorcher for the citizens of Pompeii. Mount Vesuvius erupted – burying 2,000 poor Pompeiians in a burning blanket of red-hot cinders, ash and volcanic rock!

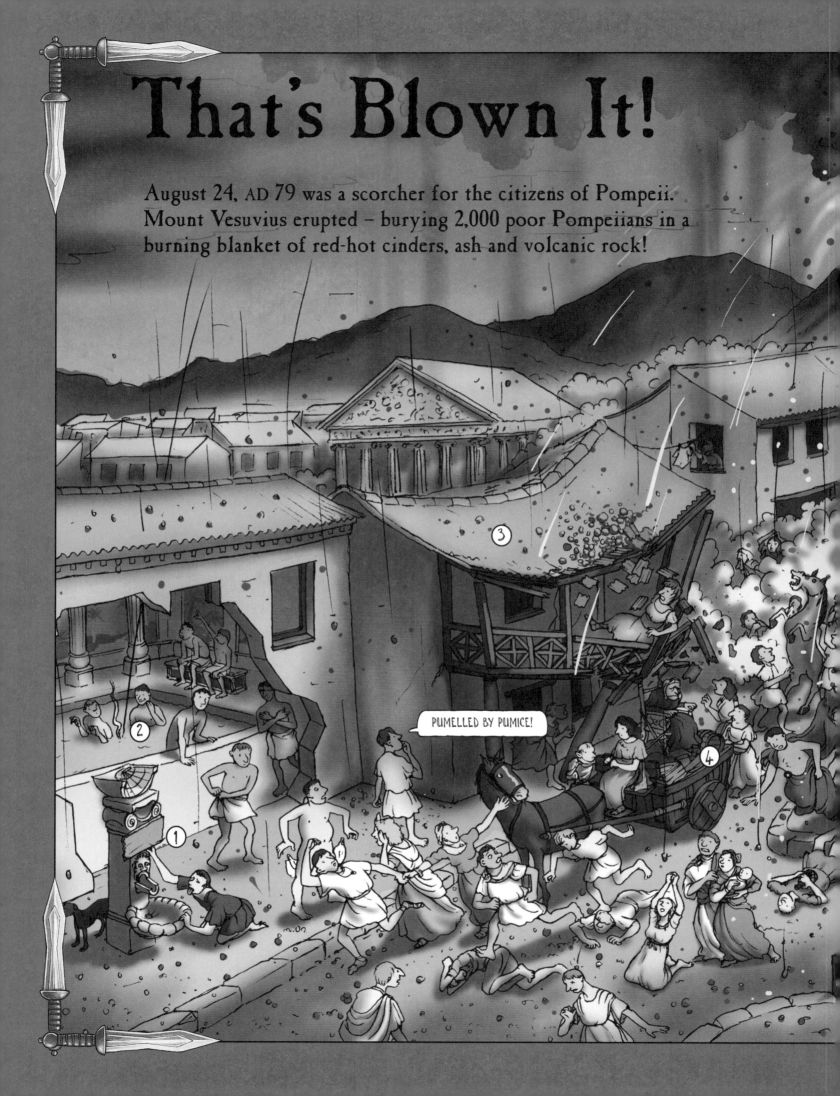

THE MOUNTAIN WITH ASH-ITUDE

1. Wells are said to have run dry a few days before the eruption. Well, well!
2. On the first day of the eruptions, Vesuvius rained down 10 cm-sized pumice stones. Great for the bath…
3. …not so good for the roof!
4. Some sensibly scared folks got away – taking their possessions with them. Even their granny!
5. Hours before the eruption, cows acted oddly. (Maybe they were trying to tell people the bad 'moos'?)
6. Despite the horrid hail of hot rocks some people just tried to carry on life as normal. Duh!
7. And when the hot ash came, it was too late to escape. Anyone left became baked beings!
8. One pet dog was left chained to a post – where it perished.
9. When the town was dug up out of the ash 2,000 years later, archaeologists found graffiti scrawled all over the walls (we've very kindly translated the Latin) – some was rather rude, but some of it was just plain daft!

Volcano Knowledge

Pompeii went out with a bang. The hot ash that killed its people was rotten for the Romans – but it's cool for school! Here's why....

Imagine you were frozen in the position you're in now – for a thousand years. (What would future Horrible Historians make of you? Would they think you were from an ancient book-worshipping tribe?) When Pompeii was buried under nine metres of ash, its people were perfectly preserved – a bit like a deadly game of musical statues.

Lava good time

The victims' bodies rotted, but the ash and rock kept their shapes. Sixteen hundred years on, archaeologists were fascinated by the spooky spaces…

CASTS OF THOUSANDS

When the ash was finally dug away from Pompeii a gruesome discovery was made. A scholar called Fiorelli found hollow spaces in the ash. He realized that these had been left by bodies that had rotted away.

Fiorelli filled the horrid holes with plaster of Paris to make casts of Vesuvius' victims. These statues show the poor Pompeiians in the last moments of their lives. Many have looks of fear on their faces.

The most famous cast is of a dog twisting on his back. (Do you think he wanted his tummy tickled?)

HOW TO PETRIFY YOUR TEACHER – THE POMPEII WAY!

Your history teacher is always going on about 'living history'. So he'll have to volunteer for this!

YOU WILL NEED...
• one fresh history teacher
• some volcanic ash (or ground up chalk)
• some plaster of Paris
• a few hundred years to spare (or a time machine)

1. Surprise your history teacher (he'll make the best shape this way) and bury him completely in hot ash. (Pumice stones are optional). Do not stir.

2. Leave him to decompose for a few hundred years. (You may need a time machine for this. Make sure you're back in school for the next lesson!)

3. When teacher has rotted to nothing, dig down to the hole and fill it with the plaster of Paris. (If you don't have any, try 'Concrete of Constantinople'.) Put him up in class and see if anyone can tell the difference!

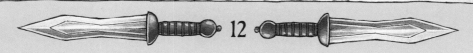

Horrendous Hellholes

Pox, prayer and poverty ruled the Middle Ages. Vikings came to slash and slay, and stormin' Normans came to stay. Wars got wickeder, knights got nastier and castles were conquered!

OF ALL THE RAIDERS WHO CAME TO BRITAIN, THE VICIOUS VIKINGS TOOK THE BISCUIT. THEY WERE A BOATLOAD OF TROUBLE AND GOING FOR GOLD! THEY GAVE THE SMASHING SAXONS A RUN FOR THEIR MONEY. THEY PILLAGED AND PLUNDERED, RAIDING MONASTERIES AND RUNNING AWAY WITH TREASURE.

THIS IS ALMOST TOO EASY!

GOD HELP US!

SOME VIKINGS SETTLED IN ENGLAND AS THE SAXONS HAD DONE BEFORE THEM. FOR THE NEXT FEW HUNDRED YEARS THEY KEPT NABBING THE CROWN FROM EACH OTHER. FINALLY WHEN THE ANGLO-SAXON KING – EDWARD THE CONFESSOR– DIED, THE CROWN PASSED TO HAROLD GODWINSON. HAROLD GODWINSON'S GRANDAD HAD BEEN A VIKING – OH SO CONFUSING! HE WASN'T KING FOR LONG, THOUGH...

DUKE WILLIAM OF THE NORMANS CLAIMED THAT ED HAD PROMISED HIM THE CROWN. IN 1066, HE AND HIS ARMY OF KNIGHTS INVADED ENGLAND AND KILLED HAROLD AT THE BATTLE OF HASTINGS.

GIMME THAT CROWN

I'D RATHER HAVE A POKE IN THE EYE FROM A SHARP STICK

IF YOU INSIST

THE NORMANS SET UP THE FEUDAL SYSTEM. THIS MEANT YOU HAD TO STAY IN THE POSITION YOU WERE BORN IN. GREAT IF YOU WERE A RICH LORD, RUBBISH IF YOU WERE POOR!

WE PRIESTS DO ALL THE PRAYING

WE KNIGHTS DO ALL THE RULING

WE PEASANTS DO ALL THE SUFFERING... AND ALL THE WORK!

MEANWHILE, THE KNIGHTS WERE ALWAYS GOING OFF ON CRUSADES. CRUSADES HAPPENED WHEN THE CHRISTIAN KINGS TRIED TO PROVE HOW HOLY THEY WERE – BY DECLARING WAR ON PEOPLE WITH DIFFERENT BELIEFS!

IN THE NAME OF ALL THAT IS HOLY, I SLAUGHTER THEE

THESE GUYS ARE SO RELIGIOUS

BACK HOME, LIFE WENT FROM BAD TO WORSE. THE BLACK DEATH ARRIVED, AND KILLED MILLIONS OF PEOPLE.

YOU MOVING IN?

OH YES...

THERE WAS WAR TOO! AFTER THE CRUSADES, THE KINGS OF ENGLAND AND FRANCE GOT BORED AND DECLARED WAR ON EACH OTHER. THE FIGHTING LASTED FOR MORE THAN A HUNDRED YEARS...

FANCY A FIGHT?

YEAH, GO ON THEN

BORED WITH FIGHTING EVERYONE ELSE, THE ENGLISH FOUGHT EACH OTHER... IN THE WARS OF THE ROSES. HENRY TUDOR BEAT RICHARD III AND THE MISERABLE MIDDLE AGES WERE OVER AT LAST!

HE ALWAYS WAS A THORN IN MY SIDE!

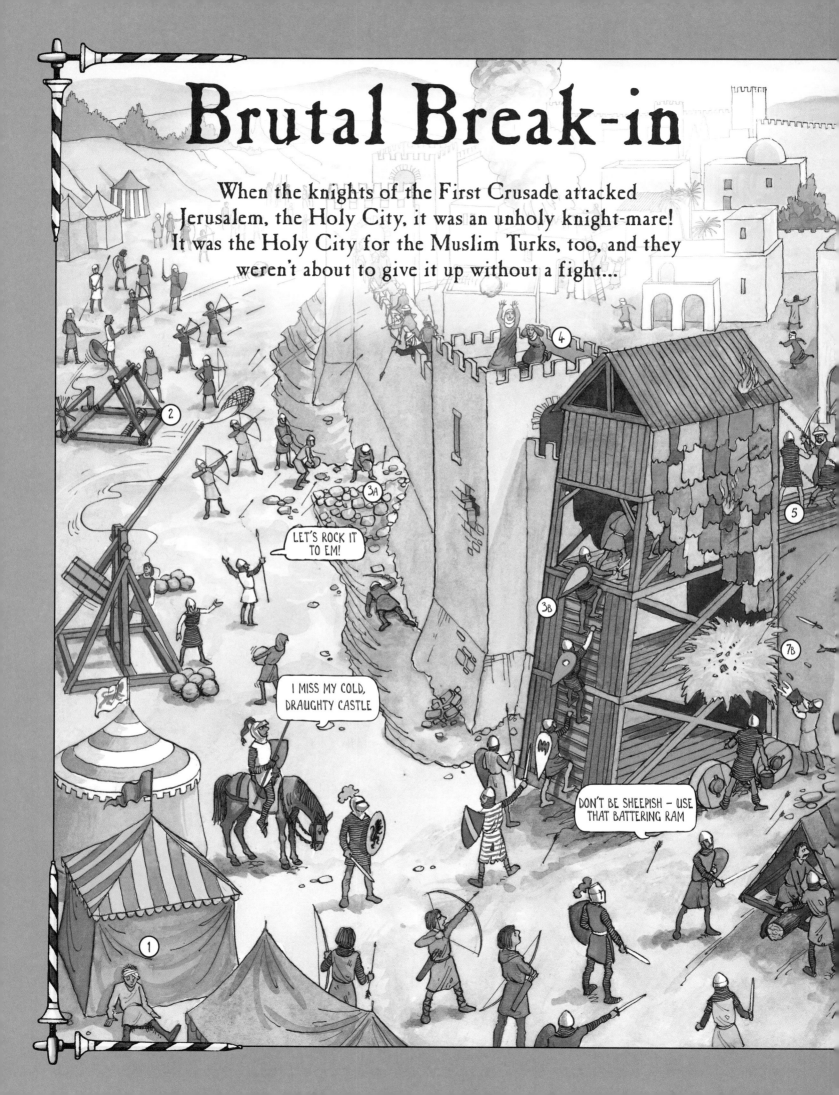

ASSAULTED AND VINEGARED

1. By the time the Crusaders reached Jerusalem, they were hot, stinky – and starving! Some collapsed with exhaustion.

2. The Crusaders fired a hail of arrows and catapult shots at the city.

3. The city walls were surrounded by a ditch, so the attackers had to fill it with stones (3A) to get their siege tower (3B) close to the walls. You could say it was a last ditch attempt…

4. The crackpot Crusaders saw two women on the walls and thought they were about to cast a spell, so they fired a rock at the women… splat!

5. A drawbridge was lowered from the siege tower and crazy Crusaders stormed out onto the wall.

6. Big bales of straw couldn't stop the Crusaders battering down the city walls.

7. The Muslim defenders shot balls filled with deadly chemicals (7A). These exploded and set fire to the siege tower. Only well-aimed buckets of vinegar could put these fierce flames out (7B).

8. Once in the city, the Crusaders killed everyone and stole their stuff. It was a case of slash and carry!

Holy and Horrid

You wouldn't want to be caught up in the cruel Crusades. It meant years and years of troubled knights!

After the Crusaders captured Jerusalem in 1099, they set up their own kingdom in the Holy Land. The Muslims were desperate to get their land back, so the two sides fought for the next 200 years. There must have been a LOT of sleepless knights!

BAAARMY ARMY

The Crusaders besieged a castle in 1099, and ended up feeling sheepish. The Muslims inside had a flock of sheep with them. As night fell, the Muslims let a few go. The starving Crusaders couldn't resist the chance of fresh lamb chops, so they chased after the sheep... and the besieged Muslims escaped! In the morning, the Crusaders broke into the castle and got a baaa-d surprise!

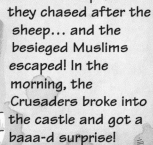

THEY'VE REALLY PULLED THE WOOL OVER OUR EYES!

DID YOU KNOW...?

The Crusaders' enemy, Saladin, wasn't quite as mean as the Crusaders made him out to be. He once besieged a castle where a wedding was going on – but agreed not to fire rocks at the tower where the newlyweds were staying. That would have been a crushing end to their day!

THE CRASHIN' ASSASSINS

You may have heard of assassins – fighters who sneak up in secret to murder their enemies? Well, the word 'assassin' was originally the name of a gruesome group who scared the wits out of even the cruellest of Crusaders.

The Assassins' leader was called the Old Man of the Mountains. One day he decided to show the Crusaders just how loyal – and lethal – his men could be. So he invited one Crusader leader, Henry of Champagne, to the Assassins' castle.

SEE HOW OBEDIENT THEY ARE

THEY MAKE ME A BIT JUMPY

WHEEEE!

The Old Man pointed to two men on the castle walls, raised his hand – and the two men jumped to their deaths.

Not long afterwards, Henry had an Assassin-style accident himself. He was standing at a window in his castle when he tripped and fell to his death. Was the clumsy Crusader just showing how loyal he was?

WANT TO SEE FIVE MEN CHOP THEIR OWN HEADS OFF WITH A SPADE?

NO THANKS – I DON'T DIG IT!

In-tents Trouble

The Muslims' top leader, Saladin, tricked the Crusaders into attacking, then surrounded them!

The crazy Crusaders marched out to fight without carrying enough water. Many fainted from heat and thirst before the battle even began.

The Crusaders made a last stand around the tent of their leader, King Guy. But it was too 'tents' for him and the tent tumbled. (Maybe Guy tripped over a guy rope.)

Saladin's men killed all the Templars and Hospitallers (types of knights). Not very hospitable!

Any Crusaders who went hunting for wells and water were hunted down themselves.

The night before the battle, the Muslims banged drums and cymbals and blew trumpets to keep their enemy awake.

LOGS IN A BOG

During the siege of Jerusalem, the Crusaders needed wood to build siege towers. The trouble was, the Muslims had cut down all the trees to stop them doing just that. Desperate to find wood, the Crusaders had to search high and low for supplies. One day, a Crusader leader called Tancred led his men off to find wood. They had no luck at all – until Tancred needed to go the loo. He had dreadful diarrhoea so he had no choice but to rush into the nearest cave... where he found a huge pile of logs. Timber!

I "WOODEN" GO IN THERE IF I WERE YOU- PHEW!

Acre and pains

The Crusaders managed to hang on in the Holy Land until 1291. But a new force arose – the mean and mighty Mamelukes. They wanted to end the Crusaders' hateful Holy Land holiday … by killing the lot of them! Soon, only the port of Acre was in Crusader hands. But once the Mamelukes broke in, they killed everyone inside.

TIME TO CUT OUR LOSSES

I'D LEG IT – IF I COULD

The Crusades had finally been crossed out!

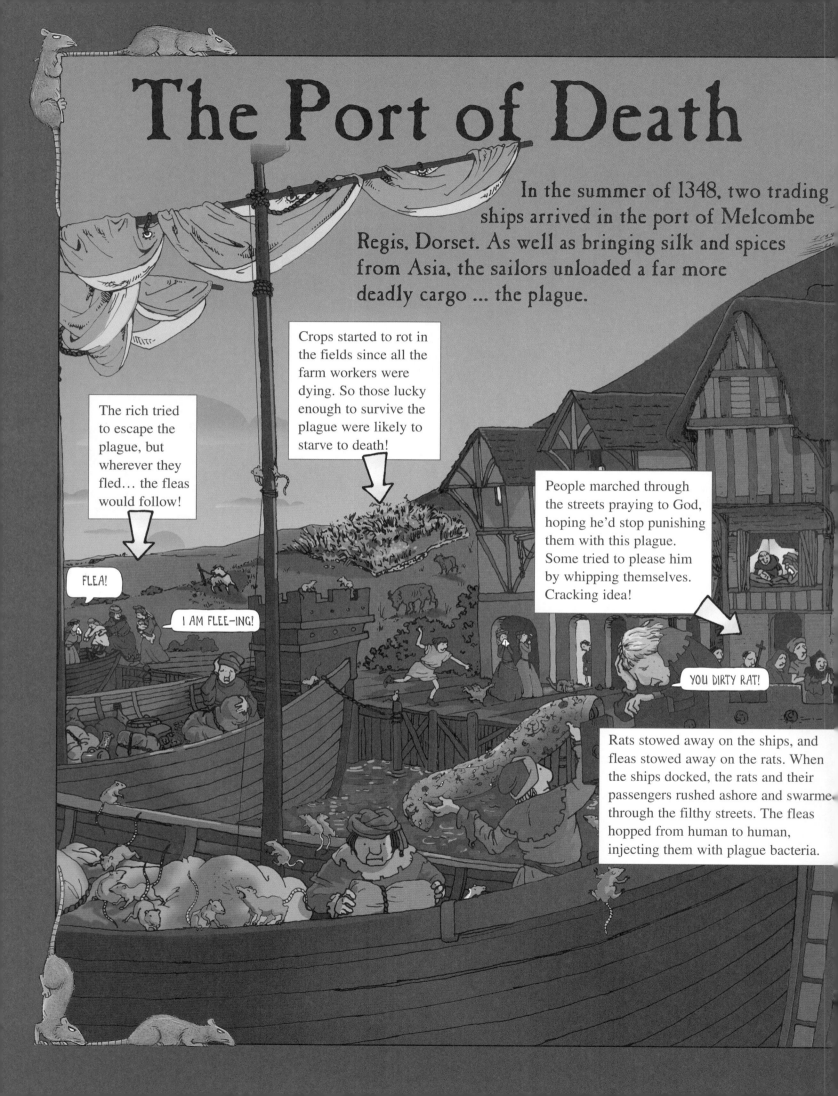

Potty Plague

In the Middle Ages, people suffered from all kinds of deadly and disgusting diseases. But nothing could have prepared them for the bubonic plague, a terrible sickness known as the Black Death...

What Happened...

In 1347, Mr Death strolled through Europe with his scythe, mowing down some and missing others. Swish! Swish! In 1348, he sailed across the Channel to the British Isles. The terrified people never knew who was going to be next.

These swellings – called 'buboes' – began to ooze with blood and pus. Purple-black blotches appeared on the skin where blood had dried underneath, and you smelled absolutely revolting! Swell – Spit – Smell – Swish! You were gone.

Mr Death's 'scythe' was the 'bubonic plague'. It was called the Black Death because of the dark blotches it made on victims' skin. Dead bodies began to pile up like chopped straw into a haystack. They were loaded on carts, dropped into pits – or, in Avignon in France, thrown in the river.

HELLO DEAR, CATCH ANYTHING?

Some people who caught the plague had a resistance to it so they recovered. Others ran away from the towns into the countryside. Rich people with country houses could do this. The poor had to stay at home... and die.

Barmy Blaming

People mistakenly believed that you could catch the plague by...
- looking at a victim
- breathing bad air
- drinking from poisoned wells

In France they said the English did the poisoning, in Spain they blamed the Arabs. In Germany, suspected poisoners were nailed in barrels and thrown into the river. And everyone blamed lepers (people who suffered from an awful disease).

DAFT DEEDS

Some people believed that the plague was sent to punish the wicked, and the best way to get rid of your wickedness was to beat the evil out of you.

In Europe groups of 200 to 300 people called flagellants went around whipping themselves (and each other) for 33.3 days – the number of years Christ lived on Earth. At first the flagellants blamed priests for the plague. But the priests fought back. So the flagellants blamed an easier target – the Jewish people. They found the Jewish part of each town and murdered everyone they found.

No shaving
No washing
No change of clothes
No comfortable bed
No talking to women

I DON'T KNOW ABOUT CURING THE PLAGUE BUT IT'S GOOD EXERCISE

Deadly Disguises

In Messina, on the Italian island of Sicily, people believed that plague death appeared as a large black dog. It carried a sword in its paws and smashed the ornaments and altars in their churches.

I ALWAYS KNEW THOSE DOGS WERE UP TO NO GOOD

FIRE!

In Scandinavia, people saw Death as a Pest Maiden. She flew out of the mouths of the dead and drifted along in the form of a flame to infect the next house. (Never give the kiss of life to a plague victim or you'd get singed lips!)

THAT'S HIM, HE DID IT!

In Lithuania people believed a maiden waved a red scarf through the window to let in death. One man saw the waving scarf and sliced off the maiden's hand. He died but the village was saved. Most mysterious!

I THINK I'VE GOT FLEAS, DAD

SCRATCH SCRATCH

Foul Facts

The real cause of the plague was only discovered 100 years ago. And some people – including teachers – still don't understand! They think it was down to the rats – but the real problem was their fleas. Here's the true cause. (Squeamish types should stop reading here!)

• Rats had the plague bacteria in their blood... which was drunk by fleas.

• The bacteria multiplied inside the fleas' stomachs.

• The fleas jumped off the rats onto people. The germ-filled pests sicked up some of the bacteria while they were drinking the person's blood... so the germs ended up inside the poor flea-infested human. But the horriblest truth is that it took only ONE flea bite for someone to become infected with this deadly disease.

ALL THIS PLAGUE AROUND AND YOU'RE WORRIED ABOUT A FEW FLEAS

Crackpot Cures

In the Middle Ages most doctors were either clueless ... or downright deadly. This was their kind of advice :

'Wear a magpie's beak around your neck to cure toothache' or 'Cut a hole in the skull to let out the devil and cure madness.'

WELL AT LEAST HE ISN'T MAD ANY MORE

So with something as deadly as the bubonic plague the sufferers had no chance!

Doctors suggested...

• swallowing powders of crushed emeralds (only for the rich, this one!).

• eating arsenic powder (highly poisonous!).

PERHAPS THE PLAGUE'S NOT SO BAD AFTER ALL

• sitting in a sewer so the bad air of the plague is driven off by the worse air of the drains.

• throwing sweet-smelling herbs on to a fire to clean the air.

• and worst of all ... shaving a chicken's bottom and strapping it to the plague sore!

IT'S BAD ENOUGH THAT I'M DYING, WITHOUT HAVING TO LOOK STUPID TOO

... and some mystic mindbenders!

MYSTERIOUS MEDICINE

Get your thinking cap on and see if you can match the crazy Middle Ages cures to the nasty illnesses. It doesn't matter if you can't, as none of them would have worked anyway! Does stuffing mustard and onion mixture up your nose sound like a treatment you'd like to try? Mmm!

CURE

b. EAT GINGER

a. EAT POWDERED EMERALDS

c. STUFF MUSTARD AND ONION MIXTURE UP THE NOSE

d. A PLASTER OF BACON FAT AND FLOUR

f. WASH THE HAIR IN A BOY'S PEE

e. EAT TREACLE

g. WEAR A DRIED TOAD IN A BAG ROUND THE NECK

h. COVER SORE SPOT WITH SKIN OF A WOLF

i. APPLY A PLASTER OF GOATS' DROPPINGS MIXED WITH ROSEMARY HERB AND HONEY

j. BREATHE IN THE SMOKE OF BURNT FEATHERS

ILLNESS

1. RINGWORM
2. GOUT
3. PLAGUE
4. SKIN DISEASE
5. LOSS OF MEMORY
6. SLEEPLESSNESS (INSOMNIA)
7. BRUISES
8. FAINTING
9. BLOCKED UP NOSE
10. BLEEDING INSIDE THE BODY

MYTHICAL MONSTERS

Middle Ages folk believed in a one-legged giant called a Sciapod. How did they think he sheltered from the sun?
a) With an umbrella made from the skins of humans he had eaten.
b) He ripped up an oak tree and used the branches as a sun shade.
c) He lay on his back, stuck his leg in the air and sheltered under the shadow of his foot.

THAT BIG MR SCIAPOD'LL GET TERRIBLE SUNBURN ON THE SOLE OF THAT FOOT OF HIS IF HE'S NOT TOO CAREFUL

OOOH YES

POTTY PRIEST

What so-called menace is a medieval priest describing here?

A SNAKE!

A POISON!

A RAT!

A RASH!

A BURNING FLAME

A PLAGUE!

DEVIL'S ASSISTANT

Answers on page 61

Torture and Terror

These were terrifying times. Rotten rulers went bonkers over religion and used it as an excuse to conquer faraway lands and get rich quick, marry who they liked and generally do away with rivals...

AT THE END OF THE 15TH CENTURY, RELIGION MAD FERDINAND AND ISABELLA HAD MADE LIFE IN SIZZLING SPAIN REALLY TORTUROUS. THOUSANDS OF JEWS AND MUSLIMS LEFT SPAIN, BUT NOT BEFORE FERDIE AND ISA HAD TAKEN THEIR CASH, OR LIFE, OR BOTH.

JUST CONFESS, AND HAND US ALL YOUR MONEY AND LAND

TALK ABOUT RACK AND RUIN!

AS WELL AS BECOMING A RIGHT ROYAL PAIN, FERDIE AND ISA BECAME STINKING RICH AND COULD SPLASH OUT ON ALL SORTS OF THINGS – LIKE CHRISTOPHER COLUMBUS' TRIP TO AMERICA. THEY WERE GREEDY FOR MORE GOODIES!

BRING BACK LOTS OF PRESENTS, OR ELSE!

YEAH, NO GOLD AND YOU'RE IN THE COLD!

SPAIN BECAME A MIGHTY MILITARY POWER AND CONTINUED TO RAKE IN THE RICHES. THE SPANISH CONQUISTADORS, LED BY HERNAN CORTES, HEARD THAT THERE WAS LOADS OF GOLD IN THE LAND OF THE AZTECS. SO THE GREEDY GRABBERS DECIDED TO BRING CHRISTIANITY TO THE AZTECS WITHOUT ASKING THEM FIRST. WHAT THEY REALLY BROUGHT WAS NOTHING BUT TERROR AND TROUBLE...

THIS LOOKS LIKE TROUBLE

HOLD STILL

IN ENGLAND, BIG HENRY VIII WAS THE BIG DADDY OF THEM ALL. THIS RUTHLESS RULER LOVED THE LADIES AND WORKED HIS WAY THROUGH SIX WIVES! HE THOUGHT HE REALLY ROCKED, BUT WHEN HE WAS RILED, HEADS WOULD ROLL!

HENRY'S ELDEST DAUGHTER MARY WAS A REAL MISERY GUTS AND WAS PARTICULARLY PO FACED ABOUT PROTESTANTS. SHE WAS NO FUN AT ALL, ALTHOUGH SHE DID ENJOY A GOOD BONFIRE AND WAS VERY PARTIAL TO A SIZZLING STAKE!

PHEW! WHAT A SCORCHER!

IT WAS ALL CHANGE WHEN HENRY'S OTHER DAUGHTER ELIZABETH CAME TO THE THRONE. SHE WAS KNOWN AS 'BAD BESS' AND SHE WAS A PROTESTANT WHO WASN'T KEEN ON CATHOLICS! WHEN SHE THOUGHT HER CATHOLIC COUSIN, MARY 'QUEEN OF SCOTS' MIGHT NICK HER THRONE, SHE DECIDED TO CUT THE FAMILY TIES. SHE HAD HER HEAD CHOPPED OFF – IT TOOK THREE STRIKES OF THE AXE!

OK, THIRD TIME LUCKY

THIS IS A REAL PAIN IN THE NECK!

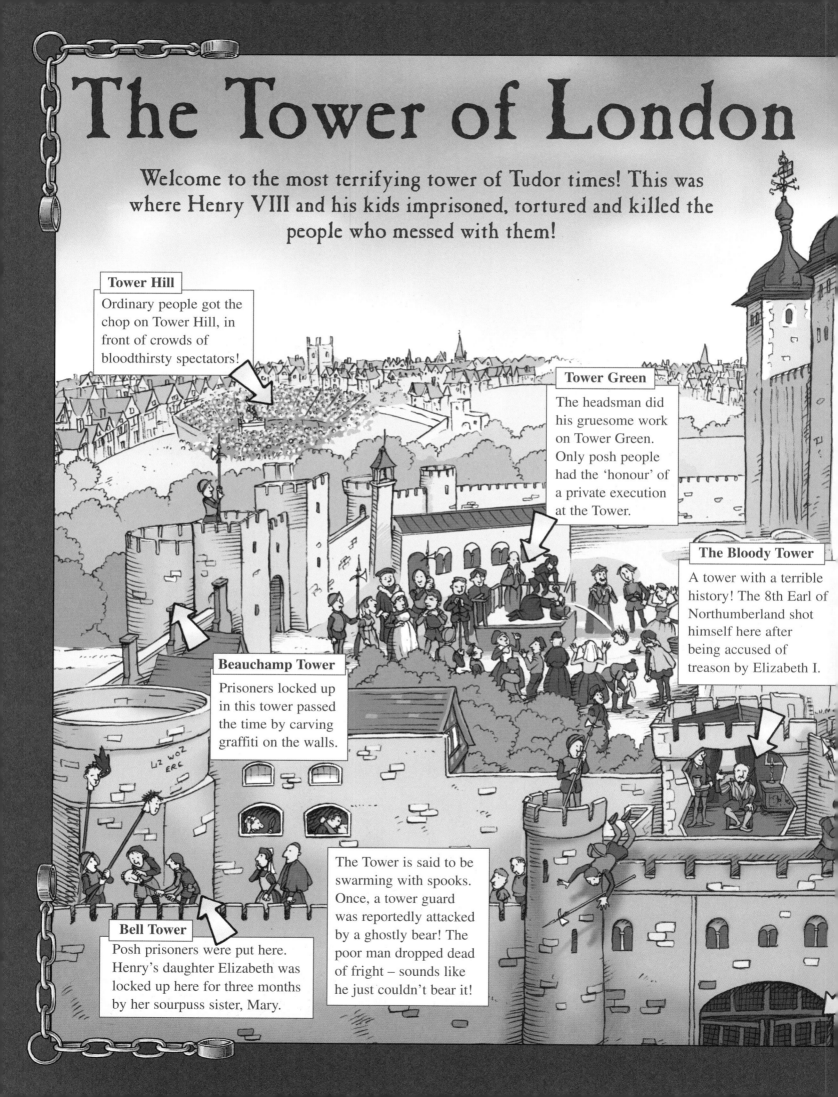

The Tower of London

Welcome to the most terrifying tower of Tudor times! This was where Henry VIII and his kids imprisoned, tortured and killed the people who messed with them!

Tower Hill

Ordinary people got the chop on Tower Hill, in front of crowds of bloodthirsty spectators!

Tower Green

The headsman did his gruesome work on Tower Green. Only posh people had the 'honour' of a private execution at the Tower.

The Bloody Tower

A tower with a terrible history! The 8th Earl of Northumberland shot himself here after being accused of treason by Elizabeth I.

Beauchamp Tower

Prisoners locked up in this tower passed the time by carving graffiti on the walls.

Bell Tower

Posh prisoners were put here. Henry's daughter Elizabeth was locked up here for three months by her sourpuss sister, Mary.

The Tower is said to be swarming with spooks. Once, a tower guard was reportedly attacked by a ghostly bear! The poor man dropped dead of fright – sounds like he just couldn't bear it!

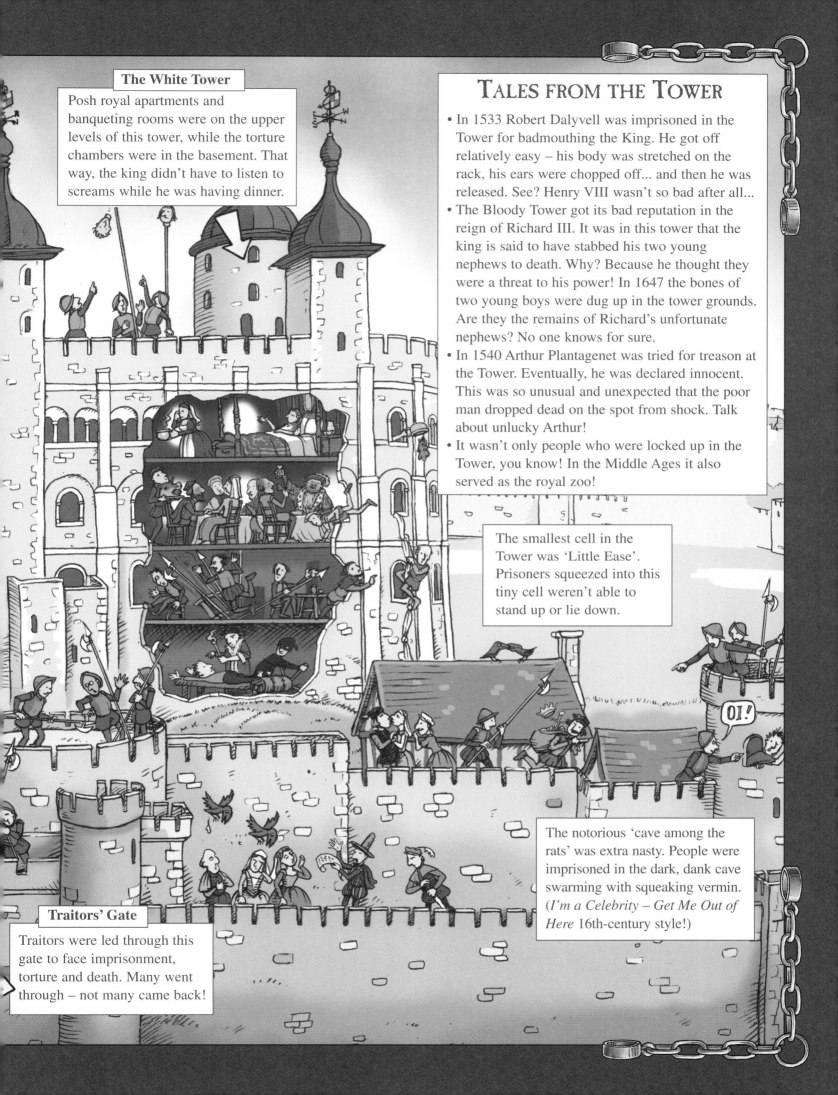

The White Tower

Posh royal apartments and banqueting rooms were on the upper levels of this tower, while the torture chambers were in the basement. That way, the king didn't have to listen to screams while he was having dinner.

TALES FROM THE TOWER

- In 1533 Robert Dalyvell was imprisoned in the Tower for badmouthing the King. He got off relatively easy – his body was stretched on the rack, his ears were chopped off... and then he was released. See? Henry VIII wasn't so bad after all...
- The Bloody Tower got its bad reputation in the reign of Richard III. It was in this tower that the king is said to have stabbed his two young nephews to death. Why? Because he thought they were a threat to his power! In 1647 the bones of two young boys were dug up in the tower grounds. Are they the remains of Richard's unfortunate nephews? No one knows for sure.
- In 1540 Arthur Plantagenet was tried for treason at the Tower. Eventually, he was declared innocent. This was so unusual and unexpected that the poor man dropped dead on the spot from shock. Talk about unlucky Arthur!
- It wasn't only people who were locked up in the Tower, you know! In the Middle Ages it also served as the royal zoo!

The smallest cell in the Tower was 'Little Ease'. Prisoners squeezed into this tiny cell weren't able to stand up or lie down.

The notorious 'cave among the rats' was extra nasty. People were imprisoned in the dark, dank cave swarming with squeaking vermin. (*I'm a Celebrity – Get Me Out of Here* 16th-century style!)

Traitors' Gate

Traitors were led through this gate to face imprisonment, torture and death. Many went through – not many came back!

Escape the Tower!

You're a prisoner in the terrifying Tower of London – but you can use your brains to outsmart the guards and make a bid for freedom! All you need is a dice, someone to play with, and someone to check on the answers on page 60. No cheating!

13 Lady Jane Grey was executed at the Tower for taking Mary Tudor's throne. How long did Jane hang onto the throne?
a) 9 days   b) 9 weeks

14 A Tower raven dies. Bad luck. Go back to square 9.

15 Walter Raleigh laid his head on the block for the chop and got a message from the king. What did it say?
a) Serves you right
b) Only joking, you can keep your head on

12 Anne Boleyn's ghost tells you of a secret passage. Crawl forward to square 15.

11 Henry VIII's second wife, Anne Boleyn, was beheaded at the Tower. How?
a) with a slice of a sword
b) with a chop of an axe

10 Henry VIII clears his dungeons by executing all prisoners. Go back to start without your head.

START HERE

1 Who built the tower?
a) William the Conqueror
b) William the Torturer

2 A kind jailer's daughter gives you food. Throw dice again.

3 Who made traitor's gate collapse as it was being built?
a) Thomas a Becket's ghost
b) Viking raiders

GET READY TO ROLL...
(that would be the dice, NOT heads, silly!)

You start in the Tower of London – one of the most haunted and horrible prisons in history. Take turns rolling the dice and move on the number of spaces shown. If you land on a question and get it right, award yourself a tasty roast rat from the dungeon and throw again. If you get it wrong, award yourself some water covered in dungeon slime and miss a turn. You need to throw the exact number to finish the game on the freedom square. Easy!

21 FREEDOM!
You are free! Free to go to school. Come to think of it, you were probably better off in the Tower, weren't you?

20 You are on the last step to freedom – but slip on some blood. Tumble back to square 11.

19 The last execution at the Tower was when?
a) 1841
b) 1941

16 You find a diamond from the crown jewels and bribe a guard. Go to square 19.

17 Colonel Blood stole the Crown Jewels by dressing up to fool the chief guard. He dressed as what?
a) a parson
b) a woman

18 Queen Victoria decides to pardon you as you've been in prison for 300 years. Throw again.

9 Two princes disappeared here in 1483. 150 years later, two little bodies were uncovered. Where?
a) in the Tower well
b) under the Tower stairs

8 You are stretched on the rack so thin you can slip through the bars and escape. Move onto square 11.

7 What appeared in the Tower in 1303?
a) chopping blocks
b) the crown jewels

4 A dungeon rat chews through your ropes and sets you free. Go to square 7.

5 Welsh Prince Gruffydd died in the Tower. How?
a) he was beheaded with a saw
b) he fell out of a tower trying to escape

6 A fellow prisoner betrays your escape plan and you are locked in chains. Go back to the start.

Torturing Tudors

Tudor times were a golden era for gore as Henry VIII's ghastly guards killed a record 72,000 people...

Awful amputation

Fighting in a royal palace had long been punishable by death. Henry wasn't so harsh. Instead, he ruled that...

Jolly jail fever

It was almost better to have a finger cut off in Tudor times than to go to jail, as they were filthy places. You could go to jail for a short sentence – and come out in a box dead from fever.

In Oxford in 1577, almost everyone in court was wiped out with a terrible sickness. Judges died, the jury died, the witnesses died – everyone except the prisoners. They lived in so much filth that their bodies were used to it. When they came to court they passed on the disease to everyone else. This nasty jail fever is called 'typhus' by doctors.

Burning at the stake

Henry's daughter, Mary, was a Catholic. When she came to the throne in 1553 she began to burn Protestants at the stake. Mary believed that fire burned away evil, so the purified souls could go straight to heaven. They looked to the Bible which said: 'The angels shall gather all things that offend and shall cast them into a furnace of fire.' To make death quicker and kinder the victims had gunpowder strapped to their legs and arms. Instead of a slow sizzle, there was just a quick bang and their bits were splattered. Very angelic, indeed!

BRANDING

It was difficult to keep criminal records as there were no computers and no photographs. So to keep a check on a criminal's offences, they were recorded on the crims themselves! A letter was burned into the flesh to indicate the kind of fiend you were...

S .. SLAVE
M .. MANSLAUGHTERER
T .. THIEF
F .. FRAY-MAKER (FOR FIGHTING)
FA .. FALSE ACCUSER (FOR LYING IN COURT)
V .. VAGRANT OR RUNAWAY SERVANT

Up in Smoke!

Who'd want to pay a visit to the smokin' seventeenth century? It was ablaze with witchy punishments, bossy bullies, and a very un-civil war. Then, just as things couldn't get any worse, 'black death' swept through London, followed by FIRE!

AT THE START OF THE 17TH CENTURY, THERE WAS A NEW NATIONAL PASTIME – WITCH HUNTING! TERRIBLE TORTURES WERE USED TO MAKE POOR PEOPLE ADMIT TO BEING WITCHES. THEN THEY WERE BURNT OR HANGED!

IN 1605, THE KING OF ENGLAND, JAMES I, MADE LAWS AGAINST CATHOLICS. A BUNCH OF CATHOLICS (INCLUDING GUY FAWKES) WERE SO ANGRY THAT THEY PLOTTED TO BLOW UP THE HOUSES OF PARLIAMENT – WITH JAMES INSIDE! IT DIDN'T WORK.

THERE'LL BE FIREWORKS!

JAMES'S SON CHARLES WAS EVEN MORE UNPOPULAR. HIS OWN PARLIAMENT DECLARED WAR ON HIM. CHARLES NOT ONLY LOST THE WAR, HE LOST HIS HEAD TOO!

WELL, THAT'S SHUT HIM UP!

IN 1665 LIFE IN THE SMELLY 17TH CENTURY DIDN'T GET ANY EASIER WHEN THE BLACK DEATH SWEPT THROUGH LONDON, KILLING 100,000 PEOPLE!

IN 1666 THINGS WENT FROM STINKIN' TO SMOKIN' WHEN THE GREAT FIRE OF LONDON TORE THROUGH THE CITY. HEY, AT LEAST IT GOT RID OF THE PLAGUE...

Cellar of Terror!

... THE PLOTTERS, SICK OF KING JAMES'S ANTI-CATHOLIC LAWS, ARE PLANNING TO BLOW THE KING TO KINGDOM COME WHEN HE VISITS PARLIAMENT IN A FEW HOURS' TIME. DOZENS OF BARRELS OF GUNPOWDER LIE HIDDEN IN THE CELLAR.

ONE OF THE PLOTTERS, NAMED GUY FAWKES, MAKES HIS WAY THROUGH THE DARK STREETS TO THE HOUSES OF PARLIAMENT.

LITTLE DOES HE KNOW THAT THE KING'S GUARDS HAVE BEEN TOLD ABOUT THE GUNPOWDER PLOT.

GET HIM!

STOP THAT GUY!

But before he can light the fuse, guards burst in and grab him! They are searching Parliament for suspicious characters – and Guy Fawkes fits the bill. (He's also the only one there, so it isn't that difficult).

It is nearly midnight on 4 November, 1605. In a cellar beneath Parliament, strange things are going on – involving gunpowder, treason and a plot...

GUY SLIPS INTO A NEARBY HOUSE...

... AND SNEAKS DOWN A SECRET STAIRWAY TO A CELLAR UNDERNEATH PARLIAMENT.

THIS IS WHERE THE GUNPOWDER IS HIDDEN. HE RIGS UP AN EXTRA LONG FUSE WHICH WILL BLOW UP THE POWDER IN A FEW HOURS' TIME ...

AARGH! I'VE BEEN CAUGHT RED-HANDED!

All's well that ends well? Not for Guy Fawkes! He is taken to the Tower of London and tortured for TEN days... before being executed in the most gruesome way possible…

Poor Guy!

Everyone thinks they know the story about Guy Fawkes and the Gunpowder Plot – but what is fact and what is fiction?

Here are five well-known 'facts' about Guy Fawkes and the Gunpowder Plot. How many are true and how many false?

1. Guy Fawkes was born a Catholic.
2. He was the leader of the Gunpowder Plot.
3. Luckily, Guy Fawkes was caught just before he blew up James and his Parliament.
4. He was tortured and betrayed his friends.
5. Guy Fawkes was burned on a bonfire.

Answers: False! False! False! False! And... false!

HERE'S HOW IT REALLY HAPPENED...

1 Guy (or Guido as he was christened) was brought up a Protestant. When he was ten years old, his new stepfather (Denis Bainbridge) taught him to follow the Catholic religion. The Catholics had already tried to get rid of Elizabeth I (with a little help from foreign friends and poisonous plots). James was just another Protestant monarch to be got rid of – nothing personal!

2 The leader of the Gunpowder Plot was Robert Catesby. Guy was fighting as a soldier for the Spanish army when the plot was first dreamt up. He was smuggled back into England to help – probably because he was an explosives expert.

3 Guy was caught at least 12 hours before Parliament was due to meet the king. And it wasn't 'luck'. The soldiers who caught Guy had been tipped off and were searching for explosives when they found him there. King James had been warned to keep away and was never in any danger.

4 Guy was tortured on the rack for two days before he even gave his real name. It took another two days before he confessed to the plot. It was six more days before he named any other plotters. By this time, the others had been hunted down, arrested or killed. They had been betrayed – but not by good old Guy.

5 Guy was guilty of 'treason', a crime against the king – burning was only used to punish crimes against the Church. As an example to others, an execution for treason was super-savage. After hanging the victim for a few moments, he was cut down and cut open. His guts were thrown onto a fire before he was beheaded and cut into quarters.

But Guy cheated! When the rope was put round his neck, Guy jumped off the ladder so that his neck broke. He was dead when they cut him open. Bet the executioner was dead disappointed.

I'M GUTTED

SO AM I

DAFT DEEDS What did the rest of the plotters do when their scheme was rumbled? They panicked and high-tailed it for the north of England!

Holed up in a house in Staffordshire, some bright spark decided to dry out some damp gunpowder in front of the fire. So yes, the gunpowder plot really did end with a bang!

While they were bandaging their wounds, the local sheriff and his soldiers showed up to arrest them all.

By 27 January 1606, all of the thirteen plotters were either captured or dead. The live ones were hung, drawn and quartered.

WICKED WORDSEARCH
Can you find the slimy Stuart words listed below in the wordsquare?

T	P	Q	N	S	C	I	L	O	H	T	A	C
Y	O	E	H	U	B	S	H	C	T	K	I	S
W	A	L	T	E	R	R	A	L	E	I	G	H
Y	I	E	P	O	L	C	S	I	H	V	W	T
C	P	G	V	R	H	A	L	D	P	C	N	P
U	F	W	U	M	E	X	G	I	Q	S	A	H
M	R	I	A	Y	O	D	O	U	Z	M	S	L
B	W	T	K	C	F	X	W	F	G	O	I	R
L	O	C	Z	I	R	A	C	O	T	K	V	L
I	X	H	P	S	T	F	W	L	P	I	M	T
R	F	E	I	H	C	R	E	K	D	N	A	H
E	G	S	E	W	P	A	C	O	E	G	U	I
P	I	C	K	P	O	C	K	E	T	S	L	G

WALTER RALEIGH   CATHOLICS
SMOKING   GUNPOWDER PLOT
GUY FAWKES   PICKPOCKETS
WITCHES   HANDKERCHIEF

Answers on page 61

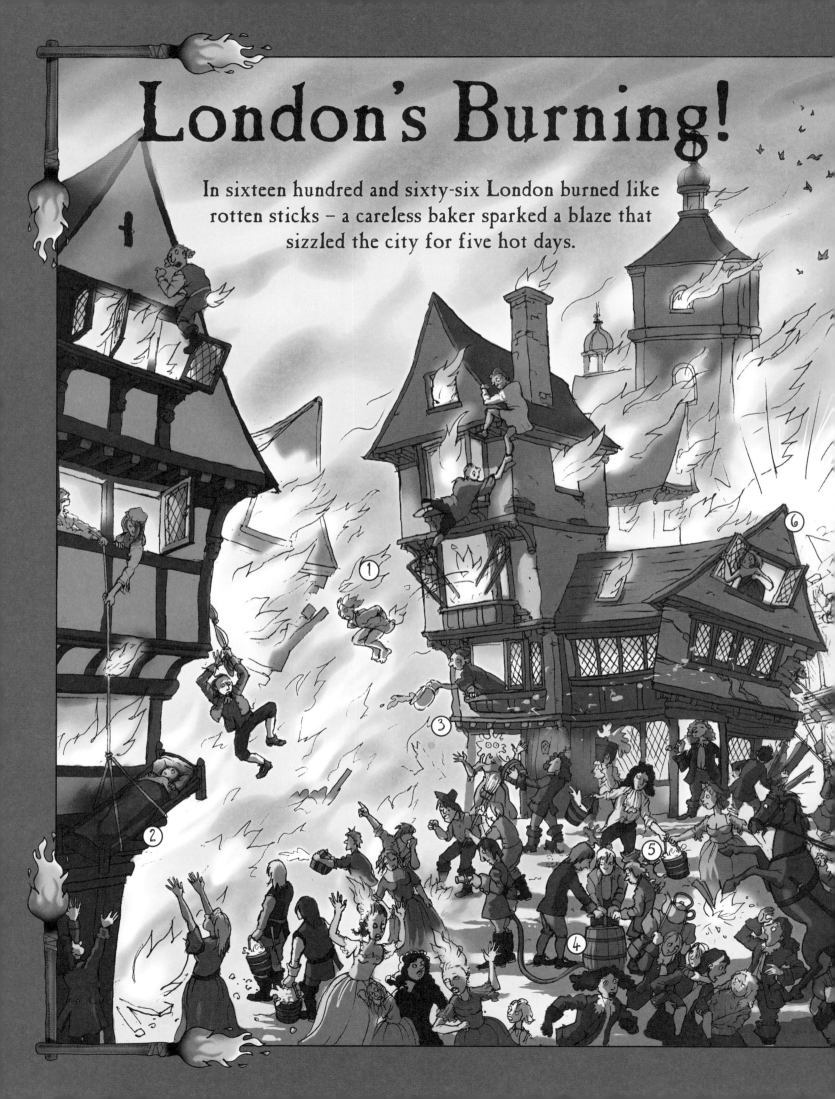

London's Burning!

In sixteen hundred and sixty-six London burned like
rotten sticks – a careless baker sparked a blaze that
sizzled the city for five hot days.

Sizzling City

1. Tongues of fire licked across the narrow streets.
2. Saving elderly or sick relatives was almost as dicey as saving your own skin.
3. "Pour on water"! How about a potty full of pee?
4. "Fetch the engines!" – there weren't any fire engines, just a few wimpy little handpumps.
5. King Charles II himself rolled up his sleeves and helped fight the fire. Three cheers for Charlie!
6. Explosions boomed as the fire reached riverside warehouses stacked with brandyand oil.
7. St Paul's Cathedral raged like a Roman candle. One witness wrote that its 'stones exploded like grenades'. The lead from its roof melted…
8. …then crept into the crypt and sploshed down the narrow streets, like a murderous river of red-hot metal.
9. Fleeing families grabbed what they could. Some struggled with musical instruments, like these virginals (an early kind of piano)…
10. …while others grabbed their pets to save them from getting poached!
11. No one wants a pigeon to come home when it's on fire! Samuel Pepys wrote in his famous diary that he saw pigeons flapping about 'till they burned their wings and fell down.'

Blaze and Blame

First plague and now fire! Was it a foul French plot, an angry Almighty – or just terrible town planning?

The first week of September 1666 was a trough one for Londoners. Thousands had died in the plague of the year before – and now, in the space of a few days, most of the City had gone up in smoke. An astonishing 100,000 people were made homeless.

FOREIGN FIRESTARTERS?

On the right is the story of how the fire really started. But did you know that the people of London blamed French spies for starting the fire? Whenever they met a Frenchman in the street they would attack him! Several innocent foreigners were dragged in front of magistrates and charged with starting the fire. Then the son of a French watchmaker confessed! No one knows why. The baker (where the fire had started) said the watchmaker could not have got into the bakery – so he couldn't have had a 'hand' in it.

SO... What did the magistrate do with this unfortunate Frenchman?

ADIEU ENGLAND

1. Sent him back to France.

2. Put him in jail so the mob couldn't take their raging revenge on him.

ADIEU MOB!

ADIEU MAGISTRATE

3. Set him free.

ADIEU LIFE

4. Hanged him anyway.

Answer: 4. The man was hanged even though he could not possibly have been to blame.

A TOAST TO THE KING

How did the fire begin?
This is the story usually told...

1 On the evening of 1 September, a little boy crept into Thomas Farynor's bakery, to steal a loaf. The baker swung round quickly, scattering ashes from his oven over the wooden floor.

OI! LEAVE OFF MY LOAF!

2 The shop caught fire. Sparks spread the fire to the next street. Soon, half of London was ablaze.

SOMEONE SHOULD WARN THE KING!

3 The king himself set off to join the fire-fighters. He ended up blackened by smoke and soaked with water, he avoided a royal stewing ... and he won huge popularity with the people of London.

YAY!

4 So did his final action...

YAY!

AND HERE IS A PURSE OF 100 GUINEAS FOR THE BRAVE FIRE-FIGHTERS!

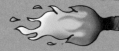

It's Criminal!

With all the riots and robbery, you wouldn't want to get caught up in the evil 18th century. There were painful punishments for pirates and hangings for highwaymen. Even the poor were revolting and the posh had a job hanging onto their heads!

VICIOUS PIRATES RULED THE HIGH SEAS. BLACKBEARD WAS THE FIERCEST PIRATE OF THEM ALL! WHEN HE WAS CAUGHT BY THE BRITS HE REFUSED TO SURRENDER. HE WAS SHOT AND STABBED 25 TIMES BEFORE THEY CUT OF HIS HEAD AND HUNG IT FROM THE SHIP'S BOWSPRIT.

I GUESS THIS IS WHAT YOU CALL A FINAL BOW

BACK ON LAND A LOT OF POOR PEOPLE HAD TO TURN TO CRIME TO SURVIVE — LIKE THE FOUL BUT FAMOUS HIGHWAYMAN DICK TURPIN. EVENTUALLY, HE WAS HANGED FOR MURDER AND ROBBERY.

YOUR MONEY OR MY LIFE... WAIT, THAT CAN'T BE RIGHT

WHAT A TURNIP!

AFTER AMERICA BECAME INDEPENDENT, THE BRITS HAD TO STOP SENDING THEIR CROOKS THERE. SO THEY PACKED THEM OFF TO AUSTRALIA INSTEAD. LIFE WAS GRIM FOR CONVICTS...AND THE JOURNEY TO OZ WAS TOTALLY TREACHEROUS.

IT'S A BAD HEAD OF STATE DAY

IN FRANCE, THE WORKERS REBELLED AND EVENTUALLY KING LOUIS XVI AND HIS QUEEN, MARIE ANTOINETTE, WERE EXECUTED IN PARIS ON THE GUILLOTINE. THEIR CRIME? BEING TOO POSH!

IN THE REVOLTING RIOT THAT FOLLOWED, A BLOKE CALLED NAPOLEON TOOK OVER IN FRANCE, AND STARTED A PUNISHING REGIME OF HIS OWN. HE DECLARED WAR ON JUST ABOUT EVERYONE IN EUROPE (INCLUDING BRITAIN!). THE WAR LASTED ALMOST TWENTY YEARS.

Pirate Peril!

It's time for terror on the high seas! Batten down the hatches, 'cos the pirates are coming aboard!

HEY GUYS, LOOK WHAT I FOUND!

HE WON'T AT-TACK AGAIN!

Pirates weren't just after gold. They would also plunder booze, pigs, and even chickens. What a fowl crime! But sometimes their victims would leave little 'presents' for the attackers – like this barrel of gunpowder with a lit fuse!

The crew of this merchant ship have made things tricky for the boarding pirates – by sprinkling nails, butter and peas on deck. (This was one time when it was OK to 'pea' on deck.)

Poisonous Pirates...

Pirates and highwaymen are the heroes of legend. But in real life, they were rogues and rotters...

The 1700s were great times for pirates and highwaymen. These vicious criminals (men and women) would torture, wound or kill to get their hands on other people's money. Today, pirates and highwaymen have become jolly figures in children's books – Robin Hoods of the seas and the roads. They weren't. They were usually heartless and selfish, killing anyone who threatened their liberty. And they were punished savagely when they were caught, like the famous pirate Blackbeard, who was shot with a pistol, his throat cut, and his body thrown into the sea. (They kept his head to show it off a bit).

Newspapers became popular in the 1700s. So here are a few hideous headlines for you to read – except some of the words are missing. Can you fit them in? Give it a go then read all the dodgy details below.

1 HIGHWAYMAN DICK TURPIN........ HIS BEST FRIEND

2 PIRATE HENRY MORGAN .... PIRATES

3 PIRATE BELIEVES GOLD EARRING MEANS HE ..... BETTER

4 PIRATE MARIA COBHAM .... SAILORS FOR TARGET PRACTICE

5 HIGHWAY-WOMAN MOLL FRITH .... GENERAL'S HORSES

CATCHES　　SEES　　USES　　KILLS　　SHOOTS

Read all about it...

1. (Shoots) Turpin went to rescue his friend, Matthew King, another highwayman who had been arrested. As he took aim at the law officer, Matthew King stood up – and was hit by the bullet instead. Ooops!

2. (Catches) Morgan was a pirate in the West Indies. The king of England met him and sent Morgan back to the West Indies to be governor of Jamaica with the job of catching and hanging pirates. He made a good job of it. As the old proverb says – 'Set a thief to catch a thief'.

3. (Sees) Pirates were a really superstitious lot. A gold earring helped them see in the dark (they thought).

4. (Uses) Mean Maria was far more cruel than most of her male partners. She liked killing better than robbing. She once used three captured sailors for target practice.

5. (Kills) Moll Frith escaped after robbing General Fairfax by shooting him and killing his two horses. She was later arrested but paid the sum of £2000 to get free.

Marvellous Moll had a play written about her called *The Roaring Girl* and died peacefully of old age.

TREASURE HUNT

A clumsy pirate captain has lost his cash. Can you spot his seven gold doubloons ⊛ hidden in the scene?

Answers on page 61

... Horrid Highwaymen

Patchy Pirate 'Facts'

So you think you know your Blackbeard from your Long John Silver? Then take this test. Here are several statements about pirates – but which are pieces of eight and which are pieces of fake? Answer **TRUE** or **FALSE** to each one. Turn to page 61 to see how you did.

A. Pirates wore large, coloured handkerchiefs on their heads.

B. Enemies were made to walk the plank and drop off into crocodile-infested waters.

C. Pirates who broke the ship's most serious rules were left on a desert island with nothing but a bottle of water to drink and a gun to shoot animals.

D. Some pirates limped around on wooden legs.

E. If a pirate had a parrot they would always walk around with it sitting on their shoulder.

F. If pirates had treasure they would bury it on islands and make secret maps so they could find it again.

G. Treasure Island was a real place.

H. If someone was found guilty of a serious crime, he'd be tied to ropes, thrown into the sea and then dragged under the bottom of the ship and pulled out the other side.

I. Even the toughest pirates liked to wear pretty gold rings in their ears. The pirates believed that they would give them better eyesight.

J. If a pirate gave you a black spot or an Ace of Spades playing card, it was bad news. It meant he was out to get you.

SITTING ON THE SAILS REALLY PUTS THE WIND UP ME!

DON'T DESERT ME!

YOU'VE HAD YOUR JUST DESERTS

MY TIMBERS ARE SHIVERING

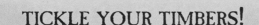

TICKLE YOUR TIMBERS! Try these on your friends...

Q. What's a pirate's favourite letter?
A. The letter AARRR!

Q. How much did the pirate pay for his peg leg and hook?
A. An arm and a leg!

Q. What has eight arms and eight legs?
A. Eight pirates.

Cruel for Convicts

Prisoners had a terrible time inside (and outside) penal colonies.
And the journey there was no pleasure cruise!

Not many convicts died on the First Fleet – but the convicts who came after weren't so lucky. Ships' captains were more interested in making a profit than in the health of the convicts. The conditions on board were even worse than the scummiest school. And of course, if they survived the voyage from Britain to Australia, his (or her) troubles were only just beginning…

DID YOU KNOW…?

The youngest of the first convicts to be sent to Australia was how old?
a) nineteen b) fifteen c) nine

I'M A HARDENED CRIMINAL

I'M A JUVENILE DELINQUENT

I'M A LONG WAY FROM MY MUMMY

Answer: c) Nine. John Hudson was a nine-year-old chimney sweep. Very young for a brush with the law!

ROTTEN SHIPS OF HORRORS

If you were tough enough to survive the sailing to Oz, you stepped off the boat looking like you'd been dragged off the seabed! Here's some of the foulness convicts had to cope with…

LICE NEW FRIENDS
Every convict was crawling with lice. One man was found to have over 10,000 lice on him. (Which means someone had to count them! Not a lice job!)

ROTTEN STYLES
In wet weather you got damp – and never got the chance to dry out, so your clothes rotted on you.

CHAIN REACTIONS
Convicts were kept locked in cages below decks, chained together.

GRIM GRUB
Dinner was a piece of hardtack (biscuit), maybe a scrap of salted beef, and water… oh and the maggots that had helped themselves to your food first.

TOILET TROUBLE
You had to use a bucket for a loo. If the sea was stormy, the contents sploshed about… so the floor was always swimming in poo, wee and sick .

DEADLY STRAW DRAW

Convicts in the grisly Norfolk Island penal colony worked out a desperate and truly horrible way to escape from their island hell. They would draw straws for two prizes. All the straws were the same length except for two … one shorter and one longer.

The one who drew the long straw won first prize – he was murdered by the one who drew the short straw, and so got to leave the island straight away… in a coffin! The one with the short straw got off the island too because he was sent to Sydney to be tried, and usually hanged, for murder.

This isn't quite as daft as it sounds. Most convicts were devout Christians and the Church teaches that suicide is a sin. With the prize draw system, someone else killed you, and you had a good chance of going to heaven. Far better than staying in a living hell.

Hideous Hangouts

After they'd bashed Napoleon in 1805, the Brits' empire got bigger and beastlier. Foul factories made people richer, but work was harsh. What with rogues, ruffians and rats running the streets, life really stank for "the great unwashed"...

THE BEASTLY BATTLE OF TRAFALGAR WAS BETWEEN ADMIRAL NELSON AND NAPOLEON, WHO WANTED TO INVADE BRITAIN. IT WAS A TRULY HORRIBLE HANGOUT WHEN NELSON WRECKED NAPOLEON'S FLEET... AROUND 18,000 MEN DIED!

NAPOLEON HAS BEEN DE-FLEETED!

IN 1858, LONDONERS HAD A STINKING SUMMER. THE THAMES HAD BECOME PACKED WITH POO AS SEWAGE DRAINED INTO IT. EVEN POSH MPS FLED THE STINKY HOUSES OF PARLIAMENT.

I SAY, WHAT A FRIGHTFUL STENCH

VOTE ME

THE INDUSTRIAL REVOLUTION MEANT FACTORIES WERE SPRINGING UP EVERYWHERE – BUT THAT WASN'T ALWAYS SO GREAT FOR THE WORKERS. KIDS HAD A MISERABLE TIME SLAVING IN THE FIERCE FACTORIES, SOMETIMES GETTING DAILY BEATINGS.

AND AS IF BEATINGS WERE NOT BAD ENOUGH, 19TH CENTURY NAUGHTY KIDS COULD ALSO GET SUSPENDED – SUSPENDED BY THE NECK UNTIL DEAD! ANYONE UNDER SEVEN WAS TOO YOUNG TO BE HANGED. THE PROBLEM WAS THERE WERE NO BIRTH CERTIFICATES UNTIL 1837. SO HOW DID YOU KNOW IF A PERSON WAS TOO YOUNG TO HANG?

WE DON'T WANT CHILDREN THINKING THEY CAN GET AWAY WITH CRIMES

I'M ONLY SIX YEARS OLD, YOUR HONOUR

OH... OK... OFF YOU TROT THEN, LITTLE CHAP

IN FACT, EVERY DAY LIFE WAS PRETTY NASTY – UNLESS YOU WERE LOADED. THE SLUMS WERE FULL OF DIRT AND DISEASE, AND THE VICTORIAN POOR WERE KNOWN AS 'THE GREAT UNWASHED'. THEY WERE REALLY SLUMMING IT!

WHEN I GROW UP, I WANT TO GO TO JAIL

Slum Trouble

Victorian slums like this London 'rookery' were crowded with poor people. They had to do horrible things just to survive – so the slums soon became crammed with crime.

Buildings in slums were often badly made. Many shops fell down under the weight of their huge signs! But a collapsed building could mean rich pickings for the poor.

Stolen goods were taken to 'rag and bone' shops where they'd be swapped for cash.

Everyone's muck got washed into a gutter in the middle of the road. People drank from it too!

WELL THAT'S ONE LESS SHOP I OWE

PLENTY MORE WHERE THAT CAME FROM!

Dog poo (or 'pure') could make you money! Tanners bought it to treat leather. Yuckily, it took a lot of poo to make a penny!

Some Victorians visited the rookeries to see what they were really like. This one should look behind him!

Crooked Crim-talk

Victorian villains had their own language. A bit like a secret code, it was made up of backwards words, rhymes and just plain peculiar phrases.

Crims called themselves 'trasseno'. What would you say to a trasseno if he (or she) asked you these questions? Would you answer "Yes" or "No"? Be careful! Give the wrong answer to an untrustworthy trass and something very nasty could happen to you…

WOULD YOU LIKE ME TO NAIL YOUR BROKEN DOOR FOR YOU?

No! To 'nail' something is to nick it. Doors were good for sleeping on. Propped up on a few bricks, a door would keep you off the damp floor (but not high enough to keep the rats off you!).

SHALL I GIVE YOU THIS FINNY?

Yes! Well, maybe…. A 'finny' was a five pound note, but be careful because a trasseno might try to give you some 'flash' money – a worthless bit of paper. You could be hanged for copying money, so forgers made notes that looked like money, but with 'Bank of Engraving' on them instead of 'Bank of England'.

FANCY A CHAT?

No! A 'chat' was a louse that crawled about on your body. Yuk!

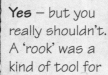

COULD YOU USE MY ROOK TO DIVE AN AREA?

Yes – but you really shouldn't. A 'rook' was a kind of tool for forcing windows or doors. 'Area diving' meant breaking into the lower ground floor of a posh townhouse and stealing goods from it.

AM I A NAMMO?

No! 'Nammo' should really be spelled 'namow' because it meant 'woman' (spelled backwards). Most back-slang words have slipped out of use – we no longer say 'yennap' for a penny and no one drinks 'reeb' any more. But you can still be a 'yob'!

SHALL I INVITE SOME JOLLY PEOPLE TO YOUR PARTY?

No! A 'jolly' person was one who started a fight in public. They could be useful – they'd pick a punch-up to get everyone's attention so that the 'fine-wirers', 'flimps' and 'dippers' (pickpockets) could go to work stealing unguarded purses.

WANT A RIDE ON MY FLUMMUT HORSE?

Just say **"Neigh!"** 'Flummut' was the trasseno word for dangerous. Whoa boy!

... and test your street smarts!

STREET CRIME SWITCH

This well-meaning gentleman is about to be robbed by a gang of grubby street urchins. But something else is going on here too. Can you spot the six things that have changed in the second picture?

Answer on page 61

MELODRAMA MISHAPS

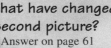

BOYS AND GIRLS! THE VICTORIAN THEATRE PROUDLY PRESENTS FIVE FOUL AND FRIGHTENING PLAYS. BUT THE AWFUL ACTORS HAVE EACH FORGOTTEN A WORD! CAN YOU HELP EM OUT? TAKE YOUR PICK FROM...LOVE, POLISH, MOTHER, PITY.

1. East Lynne
Isabel leaves her husband but sneaks back disguised as a governess to nurse her sickly son. He dies in her arms as she cries...

OH WILLIE MY CHILD! DEAD! DEAD! DEAD! AND NEVER CALLED ME ...

2. The Fatal Marriage
Isabella decides to stab herself and sobs...

WHEN I AM DEAD, FORGIVE ME AND ... ME

3. Sweeney Todd or The Demon Barber of Fleet Street
As Sweeney cuts a throat he cries...

I ... EM OFF!

4. Murder in the Red Barn
William waits in the barn for sweet Maria — who he plans to shoot! William sneers...

WILL SHE COME? YES, FOR WOMEN ARE FOOLISH ENOUGH TO DO ANYTHING FOR THE MEN THEY ...

QUICK VIC QUIZ

1. In 1817 Brixton Prison invented a new punishment for criminals. What was it?
a) the treadmill
b) the crank
c) making bricks

2. Some poor Londoners waded through sewage every day — up to 1.5 metres of the stinky stuff. Why?
a) to hunt rats
b) to collect poos
c) to find coins

3. In 1870 a new law forced every child — even the poorest kids — to do something. But what?
a) wash twice a week
b) work in the factories
c) go to school

Answers on page 61

Nasty Newgate

Public hangings were horrid affairs. But they were an excuse for a good and grim day out.

The last public hanging took place in 1869 in a square outside Newgate prison. Around 40,000 spectators turned out to see Michael Barrett executed.

Not everyone in the crowd was there to gawp and gloat. Some of them had been trying to stop horrid hangings. One of these folks was a very famous writer…

Toffs paid for rooms with the best views. Here they could gawp at the gallows while guzzling champagne. They could look down on the 'great unwashed' and get totally sloshed at the same time.

The hangman was a real horror called William Calcraft, a foul figure who caused his victims to die a slow and painful death. The crowd loathed him.

Evil Entertainment

Visiting Victorian Britain? Then don't miss out on its evil entertainments – like hangings and foul fairs!

One of the most famous executions in Victorian times was of Frederick and Maria Manning. The Mannings had killed Patrick O'Connor.

The cut-throat couple invited O'Conner, a rich moneylender, to their house for a meal so that they could rob him. First Maria shot O'Connor and then husband Frederick beat him to finish him off. Frederick told the judge…

I NEVER LIKED HIM MUCH

(Thanks Fred, we might have guessed that!)

The terrible twosome buried their guest under the kitchen floor but were found out and sentenced to a public hanging.

Hangings pulled the crowds and crowds pulled pickpockets. One thief described the fun…

"Mrs Manning was dressed beautiful when she came up. She screeched when the hangman pulled the bolt away. I made four shillings and sixpence at the hangings – I nicked two handkerchiefs and a purse with two shillings in it. It was the best purse I ever had."

Mrs. Manning was 'dressed beautiful' in a black satin dress. After the hanging those dresses suddenly went out of fashion. Wonder why?

PLAYING HANGMAN

Want a job where you get to work with new people every day? Then why not become a hangman? There were benefits – a house, food, clothes, and even pay. The hangman was also allowed to keep his victim's clothes. This happened even if the victim got let off at the last minute – so sometimes a condemned man could have a 'lucky' escape from hanging, but then have to walk home naked!

Some hangmen even became famous – like William Calcraft. His speciality was hanging his victims slowly. Sometimes they took five minutes to die. Calcraft got paid for each hanging – and sold bits of the hanging ropes as souvenirs. Talk about money for old rope!

FOUL FAIRS!

If a horrible hanging wasn't enough for you, you could always top up with a bit of fun at a Victorian fair. Dogs killing rats, men boxing without gloves till their faces were a bloody pulp – hardly fun, hardly fair! But many Victorians thought it was. They lapped it up – and especially those freak shows between the swings and roundabouts. Look at the line-up for a Hyde Park Fair of 1860 (above) and you'll see the names of some really freaky sounding acts.

the HYDE PARK FAIR Presents A SPECTACULAR TO CELEBRATE QUEEN VICTORIA'S 30 YEARS ON THE THRONE SEE: THE TALENTED PIGS. THE WORLD'S FATTEST MAN. THE WORLD'S SPOTTIEST BOYS. THE PONIES THAT TELL YOUR FORTUNE. MISS SCOTT- THE TWO-HEADED LADY. YORKSHIRE JACK- THE LIVING SKELETON. MADAM STEVENS- THE PIG-FACED LADY

Woeful World Wars

The first half of the 20th century was a time of bickering and bashing on the biggest scale ever. Bullies tried to have their way, but bullets and bombs made life beastly for everyone.

BEFORE THE FIRST WORLD WAR STARTED EUROPE WAS SPLIT INTO TWO RIVAL GANGS WHO LIKED TO ARGUE AND INSULT EACH OTHER.

YOU'RE GOING DOWN!

YOU STINK!

LET ME GO!

GET LOST!

IT'S NOT OUR FIGHT

THE BICKERING TURNED INTO FIGHTING, AND THE FIRST WORLD WAR BROKE OUT...

THE BRITS AND FRENCH BATTLED THE GERMANS...

THE GERMANS BATTLED THE RUSSIANS...

WE'RE OUT...

...AND WE WANT IN!

THE RUSSIANS HAD A REVOLUTION AND PULLED OUT...

... AND AMERICA JOINED IN

FOUR YEARS LATER THE WAR WAS OVER AND GERMANY AND ITS GANG WERE BEATEN. BUT IN REALITY, EVERYONE LOST. MILLIONS OF PEOPLE HAD BEEN KILLED, AND THE WORLD WOULD NEVER BE THE SAME AGAIN.

WHEN GERMANY LOST THE FIRST WORLD WAR, IT HAD TO SIGN A TREATY TO MAKE SURE THAT IT WOULD NEVER BE A DANGER AGAIN. THE TREATY MADE THE GERMANS POOR – AND ANGRY! ONE OF THE ANGRIEST WAS ADOLF HITLER, LEADER OF THE NAZI POLITICAL PARTY. HE TOLD THE GERMAN PEOPLE TERRIBLE LIES – LIKE THEIR PROBLEMS WERE CAUSED BY JEWS AND COMMUNISTS – AND PROMISED TO LEAD GERMANY TO GLORY.

IN 1933, HITLER BECAME RULER OF GERMANY. HE GOT INTO POWER BECAUSE MANY GERMANS BELIEVED HIS FIBS... AND ANYONE WHO DIDN'T, GOT BEATEN UP FOR SAYING SO!

HEIL HITLER!

HEIL HITLER!

NAZI GERMANY HAD BUSILY BEGAN BUILDING NEW TANKS AND PLANES. AND BEFORE ANYONE COULD STOP THEM, THEY PUSHED THEIR WAY INTO NORWAY, DENMARK, BELGIUM, THE NETHERLANDS AND FRANCE.

HITLER CALLED ON BRITAIN TO SURRENDER, BUT THE PRIME MINISTER, WINSTON CHURCHILL, WOULD HAVE NONE OF IT... SO HITLER ORDERED A MASSIVE AIR ATTACK AGAINST BRITAIN, CALLED THE BLITZ, BUT THE BRITS DIDN'T GIVE IN.

HMMM... LOOKS LIKE WE'LL HAVE TO REDECORATE.

Life in the Trenches

Soldiers in the First World War faced a mud-splattered scene of death and suffering. Then they had to go into battle! Dodge the shells and sniper fire on this tour of terrible trench life...

No Man's Land separated the German and British trenches. It wasn't a good place to die since it was too dangerous to recover your body. You became food for the rats, who loved to eat eyeballs and livers!

Death was never far away in the trenches. The Brits and Germans lobbed random shells at each other for some target practice!

There were no toilets for the British tommy in the trenches, just a good old bucket. You could make a dash for the toilet sheds behind the trenches, but you'd have enemy bullets whistling about your ears. As for washing your hands… forget it!

Trenches were dug in a zig-zag pattern. This meant there was always a corner to hide behind if the enemy attacked.

POO!

OI! YOU DIRTY RAT!

The trenches were swarming with huge rats that had grown fat by eating the bodies of dead soldiers. These riotous rodents spread fleas and ate the soldiers' rations – so the soldiers ate the rats in return!

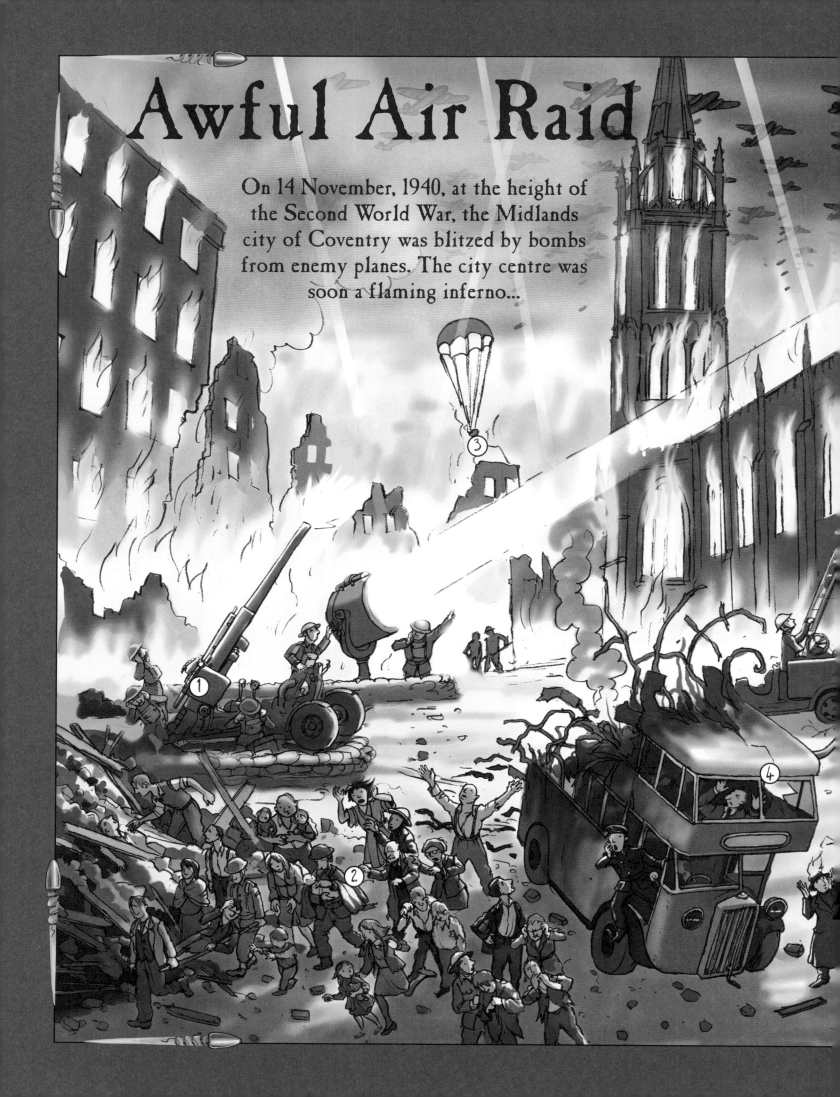

RUBBLE TROUBLE

1. The anti-aircraft guns weren't much use. Of the 500 bombers that attacked, only one got shot down.
2. Soldiers, air raid wardens and passers-by did their best to drag victims – and bodies – from the smouldering wreckage. Over 500 people were killed in the bombing.
3. Most of the bombs dropped were fire bombs, but there were also parachute mines. These exploded above the ground – destroying everything underneath.
4. Buses were used to get rescue workers to the city centre.
5. The fires were so fierce that even the German bomber pilots, high up in the sky, could smell the smoke.
6. Firemen did their best, but despite their hard work, over half of Coventry's homes (and the city's famous cathedral) were destroyed. The city would never be the same.
7. Citizens were desperate for shelter. They headed into cellars, sewers and even church crypts.

We're Talking Trench

Surviving the trenches in the First World War wasn't just about dodging bullets. You had to 'wise up' – which meant learning the lingo and how to stay lucky.

British soldiers had a gift for language – well, slang really. There were two types of slang – one used by the officers and the other by the soldiers. Look at the cartoons on this page (numbered 1 to 4) and see if you can guess what's being said. (Don't worry if you can't, the answers are in the upside-down text).

3. I'M HITCHY-KOO FROM THESE CHATS IN MY TEDDY-BEAR AND I WISH I WAS BACK IN MUFTI

IS THAT SO?

1. I'D LOVE A BON BABY'S HEAD, FOLLOWED BY A DOG AND MAGGOT, WASHED DOWN WITH GUNFIRE. FOR AFTERS I'D HAVE A POZZY ON JAPAN.

PARDON?

2. NOW, STOUT FELLOW, THIS PIP EMMA WE NEED SOME EYEWASH BEFORE THE DEVIL DODGER COMES TO CHECK OUR FLEABAGS

YOU WHAT?

4. I GOT A BLIGHTY ONE WHEN A TOFFEE APPLE, AN EGG AND A FLYING PIG LANDED IN MY GLORY HOLE

OH?

Here are the trench talk translations:

1. I'd love some nice meat pudding followed by bread and cheese, washed down with a cup of strong tea. For afters I'd like jam on bread.
2. Now, my good man, this afternoon (p.m.) we need some tidying up before the mad army chaplain comes to inspect our sleeping-bags.
3. I am itching from all the lice in my shaggy fur coat and I wish I was back in my normal street clothes.
4. I received a wound that will get me sent home when a mortar bomb, a mine and another mortar bomb landed in my dugout.

Seriously spooky

Under the constant threat of danger, it's important to believe in something to keep you going. In the trenches, it paid to know these superstitions since they might just save your life!

For starters, it was sensible to carry your pocket Bible around with you – not because your mother gave it to you, but there were stories of them stopping bullets. Now that's what you could call divine intervention!

It was also never a good idea to light three cigarettes with the same match. If an enemy sniper is on the look out, then the first lit cigarette catches his eye, the second gives him a chance to aim, and the third gives him an opportunity to pull the trigger. Bang! (Better still don't light a cigarette to start with.)

NEVER LIGHT THREE CIGARETTES WITH A SINGLE MATCH

Balloon-acy!

During the Second World War, air raids had to be the most awful part of wartime life. But there were ways of surviving them...

The blitzed Brits were especially afraid of dive-bombers. These aeroplanes swooped low to drop their bombs. To stop this, huge silvery balloons, each as big as a house, were filled with gas and floated over towns. They were tied to the ground with thick steel cables, which bombers (and V1 flying bombs) often flew into. The balloons made people feel safer but they also caused problems...

• Ever blown up a balloon and let go of the end? If a barrage balloon split, it would charge around the sky in the same way.

-THHHHRRRRPPPP

• A balloon could catch fire then land on the city below – just like a big fire bomb.

I THOUGHT THEY WERE SUPPOSED TO BE ON OUR SIDE

WELL, IT'S CERTAINLY ON OUR HOUSE

• A loose balloon trailed its wires. If they caught overhead electricity power cables, they could leave a town without power for hours.

WIRE WE WAITING?

BLAST RESORTS

The best way to be safe from bombs was to go underground. The government didn't want that – they thought people would never come up to work. But people had other ideas…

• In Liverpool, they took over underground train stations after turning the electricity off to make them safe. Police were sent in to arrest those who'd done it. But when they asked who had, they were told…

WE DID!

OH ERM, CARRY ON THEN

A TICKET TO WATERLOO PLEASE– AND FAST!

• People sheltered in the London underground too. But some tubes shut their toilets so you would have to travel to another station to have a wee.

• In London, an optician called Mickey led people into a vault beneath a bank. Mickey's shelter became famous for fights for fun and fights – 10,000 people crammed in. Sorting them out must have been a tall order – Mickey was three foot high.

• Perhaps the strangest underground shelter was Chislehurst Caves in Kent. The people of London's suburbs took shelter in these amazing natural caves. It was a like a town underground with a hospital, shops – and schools (boo!).

WE'LL NEVER CAVE IN!

Answers

RIGHT, YOU ROTTEN LOT. IT'S CRUNCH TIME!
BE WARNED — PUNISHMENT FOR WRONG
ANSWERS WILL BE FOUL 'N' FIERCE!

Petrifying Puzzles page 9

Song of the Nile: 1-feed, 2-rejoices, 3-animals.
(Women were less important than animals!)

If it Moves... Mummify it: ALL are correct!

Tomb with a View: C. Pyramids were originally covered with limestone. This was removed in the 14th century and used to make other buildings

Pyramid Numbers: 2. The sum of the numbers in each row increases by 1 as you go down – so 2 is needed to make the bottom row add up to 9.

Escape the Tower page 26-27

1a) The White Tower was built in about 1078 by Bishop Gundulf for William the Conqueror.

3a) In 1240 a storm wrecked the building work of King Henry III. Thomas a Becket had been murdered on the orders of Henry's grandfather and Thomas's ghost was seen just before the storm. Ooooh!

5b) The Tower was being used as a prison by about 1232. Welsh Prince Gruffydd was sent there in 1241 for being a rebel. He tried breaking out in 1244 – but ended up breaking his neck. Oooof!

7b) The Crown jewels were kept there in 1303 and they still are – but not the same jewels.

9b) Many people reckon King Richard III ordered the murder of his nephews, aged 10 and 12. They were locked into a Tower and smothered in the night. Then buried at the foot of some stairs and dug up later. Yeuch!

11a) Henry was being 'kind' to Anne because the sword was quicker and cleaner than the axe.

13a) Jane's husband was executed first. She then had to watch his dead body brought back on a cart – with his head wrapped in a cloth. She was only 16 years old.

15b) James I sent Raleigh for execution in 1603 – then spared him. Fifteen years later James changed his mind.

17a) Disguised as a parson, Colonel Blood made friends with the Keeper of the Crown Jewels. One day he took members of his 'fake' family to visit his new best friend. When they were being shown the jewels, he bashed his poor pal over the head and stole the jewels. He flattened the crown and stuffed them down his trousers and cut the sceptre in half! Bold Blood was caught. But instead of being executed, the cheeky crim not only persuaded the king to let him off and also to give him land in his native Ireland worth £500 a year. Now that's what you call having the 'gift of the gab'.

19b) The last execution in the Tower took place on Thursday, August 14, 1941, when Josef Jakobs, a German spy, was shot by an eight-man firing squad.

Mystic Mindbenders page 22

Mysterious Medicine: 1f – It would certainly give your ringworm a nasty shock. 2i – don't try to eat the honey after you've finished with it. 3a – this was particularly healthy for the doctor's wallet. 4h – the disease was supposed to 'feed' on the wolf skin instead of the human sufferer. 5b. 6e. 7d – Bacon fat should be mixed with wild boar's grease if you can get it. Trouble is you'd get more bruises fighting the boar. 8j – make sure the feathers are not still attached to the chicken when you set fire to them. 9c –'snot a very nice cure. 10g – there's the distinct possibility of dying from embarrassment first.

Mythical Monsters: C.

Potty Priest: A woman!

Wicked Wordsearch page 33

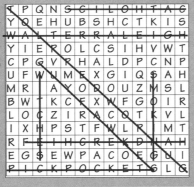

Test your street smarts page 49

Street Crime Switch:

Melodrama Mishaps:
1. Mother 2. Pity
3. Polish 4. Love

Quick Vic Quiz:
1. a), 2. c), 3. c).

Treasure Hunt page 40

Patchy Pirate Facts page 41

A. Sometimes. If you want to try this then use a clean hankie. (Snot very nice otherwise.)

B. False. Pirates couldn't be bothered with play acting. They just hacked their victims to death or threw them over the side.

C. True. (Imagine being alone with no one to talk to. You'd go mad. And teachers are still doing this to people today. They call it detention.)

D. True. If a pirate lost his leg during battle, the ship's carpenter carved him a new one.

E. Not usually. Pirates often kept parrots as pets, but they usually kept them in cages.

F. False.

G. False. It was invented by Robert Louis Stevenson in his book *Treasure Island*. He never even met a pirate!

H. True. This was called keel-hauling because the victim was 'hauled' under the 'keel'.

I. True. (A pirate never wore glasses because he didn't want to make a spectacle of himself.)

J. True.

61

PICTURE CREDITS

Cover, 4 Martin Brown; 5 Patrice Aggs; 6-7 Leo Hartas; 8 Martin Brown; 9 The Art Agency (Pat McCarthy); 10-11 Leo Hartas; 12 Paul Peart Smith; 13 Patrice Aggs; 14-15 Clive Spong; 16,17 Gary Northfield 17(t) Kevin Hopgood; 18-19 Patrice Aggs; 20, 21 Martin Brown; 22 Martin Brown; 23 Patrice Aggs; 24-25 Leo Hartas; 26-27, 28 Mike Phillips; 29, 30-31 Patrice Aggs; 32 Martin Brown; 33 The Art Agency (Robin Carter); 34-35 Leo Hartas; 36 Martin Brown; 37 Martin Brown; 38-39 Patrice Aggs; 40, 41 Martin Brown; 40(br), 42-43 Patrice Aggs; 44(bl) The Art Agency (Robin Carter); 44(tr) Martin Brown; 45, 46-47 Patrice Aggs; 48 The Art Agency (Robin Carter); 49(top) Patrice Aggs; 49(bl&br) Martin Brown; 50-51Rob Davis; 52 Martin Brown; 53 Patrice Aggs; 54-55, 56-57 Leo Hartas; 58 Martin Brown; 59 Christyan Fox; 60, 61 Martin Brown; 61(bl&br) Patrice Aggs.